CANCELLING SATANIC RESOLUTIONS

Rev. James Solomon

ISBN 979-8-88832-750-0 (paperback)
ISBN 979-8-88832-751-7 (digital)

Copyright © 2024 by Rev. James Solomon

All rights reserved. No part of this publication may be reproduced, distributed, or transmitted in any form or by any means, including photocopying, recording, or other electronic or mechanical methods without the prior written permission of the publisher. For permission requests, solicit the publisher via the address below.

Christian Faith Publishing
832 Park Avenue
Meadville, PA 16335
www.christianfaithpublishing.com

Printed in the United States of America

This book is dedicated to the Holy Spirit, the Helper of my soul and the One behind all the revelations shared in this book.
To Him alone be glory, honor, and power forever and ever, amen.

He has come that you may have *life*, and that you may have it more *abundantly*. (John 10:10b)

Contents

Acknowledgments vii

Introduction ix

Chapter 1:   Satanic Manipulations 1

Chapter 2:   Wrong Steps! Wrong Leadings! Wrong Decisions! 3

Chapter 3:   Execution of Satanic Diaries 6

Chapter 4:   Reversing the Plans of the Enemy 10

Chapter 5:   O Lord, Arise! 14

Chapter 6:   War Against Dragons! 18

Conclusion 25

Acknowledgments

DISCOVERING THE IMPORTANCE of people in the pursuit of greatness is one of the best discoveries we can make in life. It is important to note that from the cradle to the grave, we will always need people who will help us to succeed and fulfill our divine destiny.

I want to express my appreciation to some people whom God has placed in my life to assist me in my journey toward greatness. This book is a joint effort of people who have believed in my vision and have contributed immensely in one area or the other to make it a reality.

I want to thank my father in the Lord, the late Rev. Dr. James Boyejo. Your life and ministry have greatly impacted my life for good, and I just can't forget you, sir. Pastor Enoch Adeboye, the general overseer of the Redeemed Christian Church of God (worldwide), is my mentor whose life and ministry have been a perfect example to me at all times. Sir, I love and appreciate the opportunity given to me to be a blessing to the body of Christ in the Redeemed Christian Church of God (worldwide). Thanks a lot for always being there for me.

I would like to express my appreciation to my faithful friends—Rev. Kayode Kolawole of Power House of Jesus Ministries, Ibadan (Nigeria); Evangelist Mike Okuo, AIG (retired), who is always a source of encouragement to me; and to my special friend Rev. Dr. Omomokuyo of Christ Anointed Kingdom Church, Lagos (Nigeria).

A big thanks to all my faithful pastors who are committed to the vision of Jesus People's Revival Ministries and Jesus Family Chapel in Nigeria, Kenya, Sierra Leone, and the United States of America.

Introduction

HEAVENLY FATHER, WE pray that You give us what we need.

We need more than the letter this day, for the letter kills.

We want Your Word to sink deep down and be the solution of the lives who are reading this book.

Therefore, we request that You release Your anointing so that everyone will be blessed and all the glory will belong to You.

This we have prayed, in Jesus's name.

Amen!

Chapter 1

Satanic Manipulations

EVERYTHING PHYSICAL EMANATES from the spirit realm; therefore, it is safe to say that the physical realm is controlled by the spiritual realm. One problem with Christians today is that they want to be delivered (saved and cured) from whatever problems they are facing, but they don't want to prevent it. They often set themselves up for all manner of hardship and troubles without thinking of the prevention methods. I'm letting you know that there is a preventive method, and we are going to look at it in this book. After which, we will cancel all demonic decrees in our lives and be totally free in Jesus's name.

> *And the Lord said, "Simon, Simon, behold, Satan hath desired to have you, that he may sift you as wheat: but I have prayed for thee, that thy faith fail not: and when thou art converted, strengthen thy brethren." And he said unto Him, "Lord, I am ready to go with thee, both into prison, and to death."* (Luke 22:31–33)

Once demons have set up their goals against you, they begin to manipulate you in order to fulfil and achieve their purposes.

In the scripture above, we see Jesus telling Peter about the calendar of events the devil had written against him, and of course, we see Peter's response. If you have been joking or playing games with the demonic resolutions in your life, now is the time to change and be set free. A lot of Christians find themselves confused because they do not cancel demonic resolutions. The devil always takes time to sit down and put plans together that will affect your life negatively. If you don't take the time to pray and cancel these resolutions, they will surely affect you. Make this declaration.

The fact that Jesus calls Simon by name twice before warning him is an indication that He is serious. A while ago, I met a family; and at first sight, I was convinced beyond a shadow of doubt that they were a happy family. The wife was excited to share with me how her husband was a great father to their kids, and the husband equally had a lot of nice things to say about his wife. Ten months later, I met the same lady, and she told me that she and her husband were divorced. Whatever the problem was, it could have been avoided with just a simple cancellation of demonic resolutions.

Believers should stand in the gap in prayer on behalf of their families to cancel satanic resolutions. This simple prayer can make the difference, and it is a preventive way of dealing with the enemy. Unfortunately, many believers would wait to see the trouble unfold before praying. The devil does not like to see successful believers; he enjoys seeing them live in pain and agony. Therefore, if you are a wealthy believer or you have a happy home, watch out for the onslaught of the enemy.

Do you know that all the hardships you are going through were written long ago? Do you know that there are future implementations already written against your life? Today, every demonic diary writing against you shall be cancelled in Jesus's name!

When the Lord gave me this revelation about satanic resolutions, I wept because if some high-ranking anointed men of God had taken the time to pray and cancel satanic resolutions at the beginning of their ministries, they would not have fallen. Unfortunately, they ignored the preventive method of praying, and the devil's resolutions came to pass in their lives. Now is the time for us to cry and pray sincerely to God because He alone knows the satanic resolutions that are against us. Some people are supposed to be married, but the satanic resolutions against them are causing delays in marriage.

Chapter 2

Wrong Steps! Wrong Leadings! Wrong Decisions!

Now Peter was sitting out in the courtyard, and a servant girl came to him. "You also were with Jesus of Galilee," she said. But he denied it before them all. "I don't know what you're talking about," he said. Then he went out to the gateway, where another servant girl saw him and said to the people there, "This fellow was with Jesus of Nazareth." He denied it again, with an oath: "I don't know the man!" After a little while, those standing there went up to Peter and said, "Surely you are one of them; your accent gives you away." Then he began to call down curses, and he swore to them, "I don't know the man!" Immediately a rooster crowed. Then Peter remembered the word Jesus had spoken: "Before the rooster crows, you will disown me three times." And he went outside and wept bitterly.
—Matthew 26:69–75

WHAT WAS THE manipulation of the devil in Peter's life after Jesus told him the devil's plan? It was *unbelief!* The enemy had sown unbelief in Peter's heart; he led him to think that he was beyond temptation. Peter thought he was strong enough. His response unconsciously implies that Jesus was lying. When all the disciples fled when Jesus was arrested, why did Peter stay? What was Peter looking for among those who crucified Jesus? Did he not stay as a result of a demonic manipulation? Was Peter not looking for the acknowledgment that he was the only disciple that stood by Jesus during His trial? Peter's unbelief and pride led him to fall into the devil's trap. He was misled so that he can fall victim to the enemy. In the same way, the result of one's secret and sinful life will soon come to life and all shall see it. The devil uses a particular sin that is so pleasurable against you.

Notice that the same way a right step can lead to everlasting joy, a wrong step can lead to everlasting sorrow. The sin you are enjoying privately is without the manipulation of demons so that they can eventually take you to their destination—for the devil does not give anything free. If Peter left the scene like the other disciples, he would have escaped the enemy's manipulation. Assuming Peter had spent that last night praying or even sleeping, the enemy would not have gotten to him. This was a wrong step that he took which led him to deep sorrow. You need to be mindful of your steps and consider, what are the things that you are doing now? What are the decisions that you are making? Peter had no business being in that courtyard; he was not invited! He was not called to be a witness at the trial of Jesus. However, the devil needed Simon to be in that courtyard at that time to fulfil the plans he (the devil) had put in motion.

Joseph had a glorious vision which the devil tried to rewrite, so he got Joseph's brothers on the scene. He also got Joseph to expose his vision (by sharing his dreams), but God prevailed by turning what the devil meant for evil to good. Now say this confession out loud: *"Every demonic manipulation against my life is cancelled today, in the name of Jesus!"*

Joseph took a wrong step by innocently sharing his dreams/visions. The same could be happening to you. The enemy wants to push you to that point where you will take a wrong step that will eventually leave you vulnerable and with your guards down.

Are you a beautiful young lady that all the rich and eligible men in town desire? Know that the enemy could be leading you to take a wrong step in order to steal your destiny. I remember the story of a pastor's wife. The devil led her to believe that she was too sophisticated for her husband by filling her mind with self-absorbing thoughts of her beauty. She kept affirming her beauty to herself.

CANCELLING SATANIC RESOLUTIONS

She ended up backsliding from the faith and marrying another man. Some might think that there is nothing wrong in knowing that you are beautiful, but in this case, the devil carefully used this knowledge to bring down a child of God. There are some manipulations that seem ridiculous (or even harmless), but don't be deceived, they all serve to fulfil the devil's purpose, and today, all such manipulations will be wiped out in the name of Jesus.

Chapter 3

Execution of Satanic Diaries

THERE IS NOTHING that the devil plans without paying the cost to see its fulfilment. Today, I decree that whatever has been written against you in the devil's diaries will fail, in the name of Jesus!

> *How you have fallen from heaven, morning star, son of the dawn! You have been cast down to earth, you who once laid low the nations! You said in your heart, "I will ascend to the heavens; I will raise my throne above the stars of God; I will sit enthroned on the mount of assembly, on the utmost heights of Mount Zaphon. I will ascend above the tops of the clouds; I will make myself like the Most High.* (Isaiah 14:12–14)

This is an example of the contents of the devil's diary. This very entry was against God Himself—what a devilish foolishness! It's time for you to respond in anger at the devil's resolutions for your life.

You, who think you have reached the pinnacle of your life and are satisfied or content, beware! You need to stand and keep what you have by preventing any evil from befalling you, and you can do this by cancelling any satanic resolutions against you. There was a woman who had four children and was very proud of them, but within the space of one month, three of them died. Don't be deceived by your actual situation of comfort.

A sixteen-year-old lady came to me for prayers; she was getting ready to write her exams. As I lifted my voice to pray, the Lord silenced me and revealed that the enemy had purposed that this young lady would not have any kids in the future. This is how wicked the devil can be, but glory be to God Who reveals the plans of the evil one. Once God has revealed the enemy's plans, it will be in our best interest not to behave like Simon Peter. Don't dance to tune of the devil anymore! Don't play games, thinking you are wise; and don't think that because you neatly and cleverly cover up your sins, you are wise.

You need to be aware that the devil has made some resolutions against your life; he has a well-laid plan of how to bring you down. He is serious and he means business. My deliverance team and I were ministering deliverance to an eighteen-year-old lady. Suddenly, a demon spoke through her, asking us what business we had with him and telling us that we should leave him alone because he has plans for the lady. We commanded him, in the name of Jesus, to reveal those plans. He listed the plans they had for the woman as follows: At age twenty-two, she would get pregnant and have an abortion. At age twenty-six, she would get married. At age twenty-eight, she would have a child. At age thirty-two, she would have an automobile accident and break her ribs, and at age thirty-four, she will die from the pain caused by the broken ribs. We knew that this was not the plan of God for this young lady, so we began to cancel all the satanic decrees and resolutions and requested that the diary of God begin to take effect in her life. Today, the lady is doing well. She did not die at age thirty-four, and she has never been involved in an accident. God is faithful! Assuming the demonic resolutions against her like came to pass, would she not have considered having an abortion, especially since this has become a way of life today? Brethren, don't be deceived, and make it a duty to wipe out all the plans of the enemy against you. Today, the Lion of the tribe of Judah will raise a standard against the devil over your life. Heaven will fight for you. God will cancel the plans the enemy has already implemented in your life, in Jesus's name.

> *Raise the war, you nations, and be shattered! Listen, all you distant lands. Prepare for battle, and be shattered! Prepare for battle, and be shattered! Devise your strategy, but it will be thwarted; propose your plan, but it will not stand, for God is with us.* (Isaiah 8:9–10)

This passage of scripture is not talking about the efforts of just one enemy. Let the enemies write all the diaries they can. Let them make every evil pronouncement they can. Let them declare billions of curses and issue out dirty decrees; they shall all come to naught. "Speak the word, but it will not stand, for God is with us."

> *All nations surrounded me, but in the name of the Lord, I cut them down. They surrounded me on every side, but in the name of the Lord, I cut them down. They swarmed around me like bees, but they were consumed as quickly as burning thorns; in the name of the Lord, I cut them down. I was pushed back and about the fall, but the Lord helped me. The Lord is my strength and my defense; He has become my salvation. Shouts of joy and victory resound in the tents of the righteous; "The Lord's right hand has done mighty thinks! The Lord's right hand is lifted high; the Lord's right hand has done mighty things!" I will not die but live, and will proclaim what the Lord has done.* (Psalm 118:110–17)

> *He thwarts the plans of the crafty, so that their hands achieve no success.* (Job 5:12 NIV)

> *He disappointeth the devices of the crafty, so that their hands cannot perform their enterprise.* (Job 5:12 KJV)

CANCELLING SATANIC RESOLUTIONS

Whatever has been written, the plans of the devil for your life will be disappointed, in the name of Jesus. Let them continue to write their evil resolutions; they shall be disappointed, in the name of Jesus!

Chapter 4

Reversing the Plans of the Enemy

When Haman entered, the king asked him, "What should be done for the man the king delights to honor?" Now Haman thought to himself, "Who is there that the king rather honor than me?" So he answered the king, "For the man the king delights to honor, have them bring a royal robe the king has worn and a horse the king has ridden, one with a royal crest placed on its head. Then let the robe and horse be entrusted to one of the king's most noble princes. Let them robe the man the delights to honor, and lead him on the horse through the city streets, proclaiming before him, 'This is what is done for the man the king delights to honor!'" "Go at once," the king commanded Haman. "Get the robe and the horse just as you have suggested for Mordecai the Jew, who sits at the king's gate. Do not neglect anything you have recommended."
—Esther 6:6–10

READING THE WHOLE book of Esther will help you understand this story better. Say this prayer, *"Lord, cause my enemies to make decisions concerning me that will elevate me. Strengthen and energize my enemies to speak favorably about me, in Jesus's name."*

This scripture above tells us of a man who had an enemy. That man's name was Mordecai, and the enemy was Haman. Mordecai was a Jew who loved and was committed to the Lord. It was brought to the attention of the king that Mordecai had done a good deed for him in the past. The king decided to honor Mordecai, but he was confused as to how to go about honoring him. He therefore calls Haman (an enemy of Mordecai and the Jews) and seeks counsel from him. Haman, thinking that he was the one the king was referring to, advised the king to do things that are reserved only for the nobles. Unfortunately, all that Haman suggested, he was asked to do for Mordecai to honor him.

If this story were to have taken place in this modern day, it would look like the vice president being asked to drive the White House guard in the presidential limousine. God is able to reverse the decisions of your enemies and turn them around for your own good. God will promote you in spite of the accusations of the enemy. Your enemies will drive you around, weeping, while you'll be rejoicing, commanding your driver to go wherever you wish. I tell you, God has a way of reversing the plans and machinations of the enemy.

"What shall be done for the man whom the king delights to honor?"

This is a matter of favor. If the Lord favors you, what can the enemy do against you? All his plans to destroy you will favor you at the end of the day. A lot of people are still quarreling with their enemies in vain. Don't you realize that there are some enemies that are supposed to hang around? This is normal, and they hang around and are present for your good. I remember a time when some of my relatives hated and despised my family and I. Every time I visited them, they would look down on me and speak evil against my mother. Today, when I go visiting them in my hometown, I am highly respected.

Faith in Christ can take you to any level in life. It can promote, elevate, and lift you higher than all your qualifications combined. Your enemies will not keep quiet; they will be so talkative that they will say things that will elevate you. Let's assume Haman did not give such high suggestions of honor and just advised that some money be given to the man the king delights in. Mordecai would never have been promoted and honored, for the king willingly listened to Haman. The Lord caused Haman to think he was the one the king favored, thereby reversing all the honor and benefits Haman had set up for himself and giving them to Mordecai. In the same way, your enemies will unconsciously speak in your favor, in Jesus's name.

Never run from problems or accusations, and don't worry about the troubles you face in life. As a matter of fact, the journey of life is a rough one. If you are currently going through difficult situations, know that it is a normal process, and everything is in order, for God can reverse your difficult situation in a minute. A miracle does not take years to occur. A miracle can occur in a moment or in the twinkling of an eye. Your story can change in a second!

The time you spend suffering and going through trials is not important, neither are the types of troubles you encounter. What matters is that you reach your goals. You must not go through all these trials in vain. *You are a winner!* When the children of Israel left Egypt, they wandered in the wilderness for forty years, and at the end of their wanderings, only two of them got to the promised land because the others lacked in trust and faith and gave in to the obstacles they met on the way. Therefore, you must be determined to always get to your destination.

There are some enemies in your way who will not give up until they perish. These kind of enemies will surely die. You are not responsible for their deaths; they die from their own machinations. For example, some people may have vowed that you will never get married as long as they are alive. They have spoken well because you will get married, and they will die. They will be killed by the vows they made. This is similar to how Haman was determined to destroy Mordecai, even after the king's order.

A sister living in London had a long desire to build a family but all to no avail. She was unaware that her mother had vowed that, as long as she (mother) lived, her daughter would not be married. This sister came to me for prayers, and the Holy Spirit revealed the whole truth of the situation. I gave her a sign from the Lord telling her that, from that day onward, her mother was going to hate her. The sister did not believe me, but sure enough, it happened. Her mother decided eventually to leave her daughter in London and go back home to Nigeria (West Africa). The mother became paralyzed and died a week after her daughter's wedding. This year, you will rise and shine in spite of the people who said you won't, in Jesus's name.

Right after Mordecai rode the king's horse and was honored, Haman planned to do something else to harm him; some enemies are like that. It doesn't matter how nice you are toward some people, they will continue to scheme and make plans to harm you. I pity those pastors who go to beg people to release them spiritually; this is foolishness. A witch should not be asked to release anyone; the Bible says they are not permitted to live (Exodus 22:18). This is an advice to all believers, when the Lord deals with your enemies, do not relax or relent in prayers for they (your enemies) will not get tired. Some believers tend to relax after they've been prayed for and received a breakthrough.

No weapon that is formed against thee shall prosper. (Isaiah 54:17)

In other words, there will be weapons that are formed against us, but they will not prosper. Don't waste your time fighting and praying that there won't be any weapons. It is none of your business if or how the enemy wants to hinder you. You should be able to stand and eat from the table that the Lord has prepared for you in the presence of your enemies (Psalm 23:5). If you do, you will discover that, the more they try, the more you prosper.

If you discover that, somewhere in your environment or surroundings, there is a particular person favored of God, do not envy him or her. Rather, ask God for your favor, for if God chooses to favor a person, nobody on earth can bring him or her down.

Remember that, as a child of God, we have authority. It is one thing for the government to pass decrees that might not be favorable, but it is another thing to get down on our knees in prayer to reverse every decree that is not according to the will of God. A man that is favored by God walks in a dimension that is higher than the laws of the land. Some people are planning against you, but they don't know that they are actually planning in your favor.

Chapter 5

O Lord, Arise!

Arise, Lord, in Your anger; rise up against the rage of my enemies. Awake, my God; decree justice. Let the assembled peoples gather around you, while you sit enthroned over them on high.
—Psalm 7:6–7

This is a kind of prayer that comes from a heart of desperation. This is the type of prayer offered to God by a person who has fasted and prayed without an answer or by a person who has been pushed to the wall. This is the prayer of somebody whose help can only be found in God. This is the prayer of David, a man who knew how to get the attention of God.

In order to get God to fight for you, you should first of all stop fighting on your own or by your own efforts. The battle is the Lord's; the Lord shall fight for you! You have no reason to brood over the medical doctor's report. Your part is to allow God to arise and fight for you in that situation.

It is one thing for God to arise, but it is another thing for Him to arise in His anger. When God chooses to arise on your behalf, no one can withstand Him. There was a gentleman who once belonged to a secret occult group. He got born again and abandoned the group. His old friends (members of the occult group) were offended by this and planned to mystically terminate his life. This man prayed and asked God to arise on his behalf. Six months later, one of the elders of the occult group came to see the brother. He apologized to him and told him that he had withdrawn himself from those who were planning to take his life. His reason was that two children belonging to two of the higher authorities of the group died mysteriously, and he was the next in authority. This was how the Lord intervened on behalf of this brother. He shall do the same for you.

Four Muslim men came to me with an insane lady, asking me to pray to my God for the lady. I asked them to release the woman, for they held onto her for fear that she might run away. The men were surprised that that the woman did not run after they released her. I asked the lady to show me her husband, and she pointed to one of the men who brought her. I asked her to sit down, and she did. The people that brought her were astonished. After praying for her, the woman was fully recovered. The following Sunday, all the hajis (an honorific title given to a Muslim man who has successfully completed his hajj or pilgrimage to Mecca) came to church and sat in the front row. Today, that woman is one of the most powerful intercessors in our church. Along with other women, she vowed to pray for the ministry.

> *Arise, Lord! Deliver me, my God! Strike all my enemies on the jaw; break the teeth of the wicked.* (Psalm 3:7)

Cultivate the habit of being aggressive in prayer. Ask the Lord to smite your enemies and to break the teeth of every *spiritual lion* that is fashioned against you. What can a lion do if its teeth have been removed? The translation of this prayer is that the Lord should get rid of the powers that the enemies are trusting in to use for your destruction.

> *Arise, let not man prevail: let the heathen be judged in Thy sight.* (Psalm 9:19)

There are situations where one should absolutely pray for his or her enemies, but there are also situations in which the enemies should be smitten; it is biblical. All those that are after your life will not prevail, in Jesus's name.

> *Rise up, O God, and defend Your cause; remember how fools mock you all day long.* (Psalm 74:22)

In my country (Nigeria), there are people you can go approach and ask for help to kill another person for you. All the killer needs to successfully carry out the assignment is the name, date of birth, and the name of the victim's mother. There was a man who made a decision to have a brother in Christ killed. He gave the name of this brother to a native doctor (voodoo priest). These native doctors use supernatural powers to make the face of the victim appear on a magical screen. In this way, they can monitor everything the victim does. The native doctor said he will call the name of the brother three times so that they will be able to witness his death. The first time he called the brother's name, nothing appeared on the screen. The second time he called the brother's name, they were engulfed in smoke, and this annoyed the native doctor. He told the man that if the face of the victim does not appear on the screen when he calls him the third time, the man should consider himself the victim. The third time he called the victim's name, the magical screen caught fire, and they literally saw blood everywhere in the room, and this was how God thwarted their evil plans against the brother. The interesting part is that the brother was completely unaware of everything that happened. Who is that enemy planning against you? Why is your business running slow? Why is it so difficult for you to succeed?

> *Thou shalt arise, and have mercy upon Zion: for the time to favor her, yea, the set time, is come.* (Psalm 102:13)

It may seem like the enemy has been successful over you, but you will shine. Every life which the enemy has condemned will rise and shine. All those who are mocking and laughing at you will live long enough to beg and make peace with you.

CANCELLING SATANIC RESOLUTIONS

If you are among those who think that God does not answer prayers, maybe you are not praying aright. The God we serve is the same of God of Elijah. He is the God Who answers by fire!

What is wrong in your life? Is it your marriage, home, employment, or health? No matter what is wrong, ask the Lord to arise. You have the right to ask Him to arise. If you have fought on your own without any answer, fasted with no solution, and done everything possible you know to do, then it is a great time to hand the case over to God for divine intervention. Know that when you ask God to arise, He will surely arise! I won't be surprised if testimonies begin to pile up in your life; your record will change. If you have received a negative medical report, it is time to laugh because God, your manufacturer, has fresh body parts to replace whatever the doctors have deemed incurable. If car manufacturers are more reliable than roadside mechanics, then God, our perfect manufacturer, should be trusted beyond the doctor's report. God is the final authority!

It is time to take our battles more seriously by handing them over to God and asking Him to arise!

Chapter 6

War Against Dragons!

IN THIS CHAPTER, we are going to consider the war against dragons, and we are not talking about a video game or a Hollywood movie! If you are unaware of the present difficulties around you, you will find it unnecessary to look for a solution. If you do not realize who the creator of troubles is behind the scenes, you will not know how to fight back. The most dangerous aspect of life is to be ignorant of the reasons you are suffering.

> *A great sign appeared in heaven: a woman clothed with the sun, with the moon under her feet and a crown of twelve stars on her head. She was pregnant and cried out in pain as she was about to give birth. Then another sign appeared in heaven: an enormous red dragon with seven heads and ten horns and seven crowns on its heads. Its tail swept a third of the stars out of the sky and flung them to the earth. The dragon stood in front of the woman who was about to give birth, so that it might devour her child the moment he was born. She gave birth to a son, a male child, who "will rule all the nations with an iron scepter." And her child was snatched up to God and His throne. The woman fled into the wilderness to a place prepared for her by God,*

where she might be taken care of for 1,260 days.
(Revelation 12:1–6)

Although it is quoted in a symbolic form, this passage shows us some specific points. I believe God in that every spiritual dragon that has been responsible for your troubles will fail today, in Jesus's name. It is nothing but foolishness to be ignorant of the fact that there are enemies fighting every good thing the Lord gives us. As a matter of fact, he fights every good desire, ambition, and dreams the Lord placed in us.

In this passage, we see how the woman was highly protected, for she was clothed with "fire, sun, and moon." Do you realize that the radiance of the sun is a mighty tower of protection, yet Satan (or the dragon) was still looking for an opportunity to destroy the woman. Since the woman could not be killed or harmed by the dragon, the dragon looked forward to destroying the child (son) that she was about to give birth to. In the same way, the dragon of this present day is not so much interested in destroying our lives as he is interested in destroying our dreams and visions. We are just as kept by God as the woman, for (we) the children of God are covered, protected, and secured. The woman the Bible talks about here was pregnant. Pregnancy can be viewed as our unfulfilled dreams and visions. A survey on this issue will quickly reveal that everybody has great goals and big plans. What, therefore, is wrong if from the time you started making plans toward your goals, you are not seeing any achievements or accomplishments? The answer? *Dragons!* In the name of Jesus, Heaven will wage war against every dragon that is rising up against your ambition.

Since the enemy is wise enough to realize that he cannot tamper with your life, he goes after your dreams, visions, destiny, and potential. He is very determined to see that you don't reach your God-given goals, but you need to know that the Lord is ready to fight every spiritual dragon opposing your goals. A lot of Christians believe that once you are born again, the shield of the Almighty God protects you, and this is correct. However, this covenant of protection does not guarantee the fulfillment of your goals.

> *A great sign appeared in heaven: a woman clothed with the sun, with the moon under her feet and a crown of twelve stars on her head.* (Revelation 12:1)

This verse shows us the greatness of the woman and how well she was protected; yet the dragon was still looking for an opportunity to kill the woman's baby. The enemy still operates the same way today. Since he cannot break the covenant of protection you have with God, he is looking for other means to destroy you, such as barrenness, poverty, sin, sickness, and the dragons; but their purpose against you will fail, in the name of Jesus!

Don't think that the level of your anointing exempts you form the from the devices of the dragon. *Beware!*

> *She was pregnant and cried out in pain as she was about to give birth. Then another sign appeared in heaven: an enormous red dragon with seven heads and ten horns and seven crowns on its heads.* (Revelation 12:2–3)

The Bible refers to both the woman and the dragon, and the King James version uses the word *wonder* (Revelation 12:1 and 3). This may lead to the conclusion that the greater your glory, the greater the opposition. In order words, less glory, less opposition.

> *The dragon stood in front of the woman who was about to give birth…* (Revelation 12:4)

This particular dragon was assigned to this woman. For your information, the order of the dragon is higher than ordinary demons. Dragons have a greater authority than demons. What dragon is assigned against you? Do you know that there are dragons assigned to kill all the eggs in a woman's womb, and there are dragons assigned to destroy all the efforts you can ever make and render them useless? Do you know that these dragons are waiting for an opportunity to smite you if you become weak in spirit? What is that dragon that insists on making you a failure forever? You need to discover the dragon standing against your life, and then in holy anger, declare to that dragon: *"The blood of Jesus is against you. The sword of the Spirit is against you. The lily of the valley condemns you. The resurrection and the life defeats you over my destiny, success, and life."*

And the Lord will deal with all dragons today, in the name of Jesus!

This dragon knew that there will come a time when the woman will give birth, in the same way that the dragon knows that if he allows you to run around, you will get to your glory. For this reason, he is standing and watching carefully to ensure that many do not reach their destinies. Today, however, the Holy Spirit will destroy all the files the dragons have against you in their computers, in Jesus's name.

Do you ever ask yourself why most of your dreams are not realized, or your plans never work, or why you remain unemployed despite the wealth of knowledge you possess? The dragon is standing in the midst of it to snatch all your ideas as soon as they are born. He is watching carefully, so that he will be able to stop and abort every good thing coming your way. We declare that the Lord will raise a standard against all dragons besieging your destiny and success, in Jesus's name.

Maybe you don't realize that there are evil forces assigned against your life, and perhaps you have even thought that the devil is not real. Your ignorance does not make the reality less real. The devil or evil forces exist and operate against you whether you believe it or not. For example, in the USA, you don't need to believe that there are police patrolling the streets until you break the law and get arrested. The police actually make it clear when you are arrested that ignorance (of the law) is no excuse. Even the Bible says, *"And ye shall know the truth, and the truth shall make you free."* (John 8:32)

In other words, it is the truth that you know that will set you free.

A brother who came to me for advice shared his story with me. He said he was in love with a particular sister, but every time they arranged to meet, a demon will appear to him and discourage him from meeting with her. So he wanted to know if he should continue the relationship with the lady. I advised him to go ahead and get married to the lady, and he took my advice and began to plan toward the wedding. On the day he and his family were to meet with his fiancé's family to finalize the wedding arrangements, they had a car accident, and he broke his leg. After this incident, the brother decided to end the relationship. The fiancé didn't know the reason for his decision; neither was she aware of the real issue involved, and even if she was aware of the issue, she would not have believed.

Another sister told me that any time she thought about getting married, a spirit would whisper to her not to waste the time and life of the gentleman she intends to marry, unless she wants to kill the man. The sister ignored the warning and got married the first time. Her husband died. The second time she met a man who was ready to marry her, he died a few weeks before the wedding. At the time she was narrating this story to me, she had met a third man who proposed to her, and this is why she came to see me. She did not want this gentleman to die the same way the previous men had, especially after the warning she received from the evil spirit. So we prayed against that evil spirit and the sister was free.

These dragons are wicked. Whenever you are ready to get married, they will make plans to abort the marriage. If there is a particular sin in your life that you find difficult to get rid of, there is usually a dragon at work in your life. These dragons aim to make you fail at the verge of your success. People need to realize and understand that some of these odd occurrences in one's life are not just ordinary. Sometimes, the good things you miss narrowly don't have natural explanations. Today, as you declare, "Father, fight for me!" the fire of God is ready to consume every spiritual dragon and their monitoring powers, in Jesus's name!

A lot of people do not realize that the dragon is not just concerned with their getting a job, or excelling in an examination, or getting married, or getting pregnant, he is concerned about what will happen when they get these things. I met a brother, once, who could not find a job. He told me that whenever he prepared for a job interview, a strange sensation would come upon him, and he would know right there and then that he is not going to get the job. As he was talking to me, he was on his way to a job interview, so we prayed. When he got to that company, he was hired for the job without an interview.

A seven-year-old girl confessed to me that she had been assigned to run down the business of her mother. There was a power that had been given to her in form of a board. Anywhere her mother went, the board would go before her. When her mother wants to make a purchase from a wholesale store, the board will influence the seller to inflate the prices. What is the dragon assigned against your home? What is that dragon that causes you to quit right before success or that always leads you to having miscarriages? The Lord will deal with them today, and they will die, in Jesus's name!

> *Its tail swept a third of the stars out of the sky and flung them to the earth.* (Revelation 12:4a)

Though the dragon stands alone, he has a whole network. So if you think by relocating to a different country in another part of the world you are running away from a specific dragon, you are deceiving yourself because another dragon will be assigned to you at your new location. It is a network. They are highly connected. Running away is not the answer, there are dragons all over the world. Today, we will break that cord and disagree with every dragon that is affecting you, in Jesus's name.

> *She gave birth to a son, a male child, who "will rule all the nations with an iron scepter." And her child was snatched up to God and His throne.* (Revelation 12:5)

Dragons never give up; they want to achieve their goals which is to destroy our goals! Getting married or having a good job is not the end of the matter. The dragons want to destroy your ultimate ambitions and the purpose of God for your life. Believers think they don't need any more prayers now that they are born again. This is so wrong, and it is carelessness to many.

Pray this prayer: *"Father, today I pull down every spiritual dragon assigned against my life, in the name of Jesus!"*

Conclusion

FATHER, WE COME before You today so that as we study Your Word, Your presence will be made real, and we will be fully loaded with Your blessings after reading this book. Lord, we trust You will give us revelation and understanding so that the words we read in this book will have effect in our lives. By accomplishing the purpose for which it was written, we hope Your name alone will be glorified. This we pray in the precious and victorious name of Jesus!

Amen!

AUTHOR'S BIOGRAPHY

Rev. James A. Solomon is the President of Jesus People's Revival Ministries Inc., as well as the General Overseer and Senior Pastor of Jesus Family Chapel, with 38+ branches, in Nigeria, the United Kingdom and several other countries. The international headquarters for both ministries is based in Atlanta, Georgia, in the United States of America, where he currently resides.

Rev. Solomon is a man who is truly gifted with an extraordinary anointing on the subject of Spiritual Warfare, Healing and Deliverance. In his efforts to serve the body of Christ beyond his own ministries, he also serves as director for the West African Regional Directorate of the International Accelerated Missions (I.A.M.), a network of missionary churches based in New York.

Rev. Solomon started from very humble beginnings in his native country of Nigeria, West Africa, way back in the 1980s. With his team of ministers and due to popular demand, he has taken the revelation of Spiritual Warfare and Deliverance to massive venues such as the stadium domes in the major cities of Nigeria. He has also conducted a series of conferences, and organized quarterly Deliverance Night Services in the United Kingdom, Europe, Canada, Japan and all over the United States. Many have received freedom from satanic bondage and oppression at these quarterly deliverance services. He is in high demand as a guest minister in many crusades and conferences.

Milton Keynes UK
Ingram Content Group UK Ltd.
UKHW041241061224
452010UK00020B/162